CW00719933

# POET'S ENGI
# CUMBRIA

## Compiled by
## Peggy Poole

*Illustrated by Pete Durrant*

**HEADLAND**

First published in 1995
by
HEADLAND PUBLICATIONS
38 York Avenue, West Kirby
Wirral, Merseyside L48 3JF

ISBN 0 903074 76 1

Headland gratefully acknowledges financial
assistance from North West Arts Board

DTP by Gillian Durrant
Printed in Great Britain by
Bemrose Shafron (Printers) Ltd, Chester

# FOREWORD

Compiling *Poet's England: Cumbria* has been a formidable challenge. Has any other part of England inspired more poets past or present?

The brief to see as many corners of Cumbria as possible represented through a poet's eye meant not allowing the Lake District to dominate, but keeping it integral to the whole. That is why I chose to move from south to north, beginning in Morecambe Bay and journeying north (sometimes, I admit, rather erratically) to Solway Firth and the Scottish border, incorporating the Lakes en route.

Cumbria is not only rich in poets (giants like Wordsworth and Norman Nicholson have constantly looked over my shoulder), but also in history and, due in part to its geographical position, in retaining its characteristic speech, lively school of dialect poetry and its customs. All these aspects needed to be highlighted. Nor, if the county is to be seen in its entirety, could the few disturbing and controversial areas be ignored.

The countryside of Westmorland (part of Cumbria since 1974, the year of sweeping boundary changes) was seen by Defoe, writing in 1722, as "the most barren and frightful of any I have passed". It was William Gilpin who identified it as picturesque in the late 18th century. Glaciers formed the character of the lakes; Danes, Vikings, Celts (amongst others) influenced the character of the people. Today it is a place which can capture the heart for a lifetime.

Many of the poets represented here are household names; others are less well known, but all have been captivated by Cumbria. My gratitude goes to each and every one of them and to those generous people who have so willingly helped me in my privileged task.

*January 1995*                                                    *Peggy Poole*

**ACKNOWLEDGEMENTS**
For permission to reproduce copyright material:
Bloodaxe and David Scott for 'Castlerigg Songs' and 'Skiddaw House' from *Playing for England*; Faber & Faber Ltd and the Estate of Norman Nicholson for 'Millom Old Quarry' and 'Scarth Gap, Buttermere' from *The Pot Geranium*, and 'Cleator Moor' from *Five Rivers*.
For other previously published material: Pat Arrowsmith, Gladys Mary Coles, Neil Curry, Robert Drake, Kevin Fegan, Annie Foster, Phoebe Hesketh, Geoffrey Holloway, M.A.B. Jones, Kate Lindsay, Gerda Mayer, Angela Mays, Margaret Pain, M.R. Peacocke, Patricia Pogson, Keith Ratcliffe, David Scott, Kenneth Wadsworth and Virginia Warbey. For these and previously unpublished poems copyright remains with the authors.

**CUMBRIA**: Map showing main places mentioned in the text

# CONTENTS

*from*
## CANNY CUMMERLAN'

Yer Buik-larn'd wise gentry, that's seen monie counties,
    May preach and palaver, and brag as they will
O' mountains, lakes, valleys, woods, watters, and meadows
    But canny auld Cummerlan' caps them aw still:
It's true, we've nae palaces sheynin amang us,
    Nor marble tall towers to catch the weak eye;
But we've monie feyne cassels, where fit our brave fadders
    Where Cummerland cud onie county defy.

Whea that hes climb'd Skiddaw, has seen sec a prospec,
    Where fells frown owre fells, and in majesty vie?
Whea that has seen Keswick, can count hawf its beauties
    May e'en try to count hawf the stars i' the sky:
Theer's Ullswater, Bassenthwaite, Wastwater, Derwent
    That thousands on thousands ha'e travell'd to view;
The langer they gaze, still the mair they may wonder,
    And ay, as they wonder, may fin summet new.

*1820*                              *Robert Anderson*

*from*
## A WESTMORLAND SONG

Rust-red are the mountains
    And white fall the fountains
        When over Helvellyn fly wintry gales;
But green when the comer,
Who brings us the summer.
        The cuckoo calls clear o'er the Westmorland dales.

When bracken was springing
The live air was ringing.
        The lambs with loud chorus filled valleys below;
Now bracken is umber,
How deep is the slumber
        Of mountains that wait for the silence of snow.

Ye Westmorland mountains.
Ye Westmorland fountains.
        The clouds are your children, the streams are your birth:
When tear-drops fall quickly,
And clouds gather thickly
        Your calm and your hope bring new comfort to Earth.

*1887*                                *H.D. Rawnsley*

*from*
## POLY-OLBION (30th Song)

Of Westmerland the Muse now sings,
And fetching Eden from her springs,
Sets her along, and Kendall then
Surveying, beareth backe agen;
And climing Skidows lofty hill,
By many a river, many a rill,
To Cumberland, where in her way,
Shee Copland calls, and doth display
Her beauties, backe to Eden goes,
Whose floods, and fall she aptly showes.

*1622*          *Michael Drayton*


## HAIL(E) CUMBRIA

Buckabank, St Bees,
Unthank, Blitterlees,
Seldom Seen, Stickle Pike,
Eskdale Green, Sandysike,
Stagshaw, Skinburness,
Skiddaw, High Furness,
Catbells, Catchedican,
Shap Fells, Spadeadam,
Sour Milk Gill, Lazonby,
Loadpot Hill, Crosscanonby
High Street, Clappersgate,
Lord's Seat, Satterthwaite,
Black Sail, Blennerhassett,
Mardale, Dunmallet,
Scotsdike, Arrant How,
Aye Gill Pike, Ladder Brow,
Mickledore Ridge, Brunt Knott,
Standing Edge, Priest's Pot,
Millthrop, Frizington,
Hartsop, Killington,
Justicetown, Gibbergill,
Butterburn, Stotts Mills,
Tarn Bay, Wrynose Pass,
High Wray, Ravenglass,
Orton, Crosby Garrett, Boot:
each one merits your salute.

*1995*          *Peggy Poole*

## REQUIEM FOR THREE COUNTIES

Nobody asked if they could take away
for ever the names, the place I loved
where three hill counties met.
All's changed – crowds swarm
on the eroded paths, rare flowers are gone
and trashy shops are packed with bargain-hunters.
Elterwater boasts its time-share and Jacuzzi...

I envy all those early travellers who
saw the old Westmorland wild and desolate,
empty as Rannoch Moor, explored the pictures
of my childhood where mauve mist swirled
above the quiet lakes with shaggy cattle wading.

Yet the rocks remain – not all the paths
are waymarked.  Striding Edge is, so far, unpaved,
High Street's escaped the tarmac and there are
lonely places by Far Easedale and Wise Een Tarn.

*1991*                               *Margaret Caunt*


## THE THREE SHIRES STONE, WRYNOSE

It has stood through countless ages, as a Mizpah and a Guide
         To the wanderer o'er the valley and the hill,
And it tells in silent language on the lonely mountain side
         That amongst us there's a bond of union still.

In the lispings of our childhood, in the country of our birth,
         In our love of all that's faithful, kind and true;
In the memories that we cherish of the great and good of earth,
         There's a bond, dear Sister Counties, still with you.

Yes, these names will go engraven on the tablets of his mind
         With the wanderer during many a weary day;
He will think of them in speaking of the friends he's left behind
         And remember them in countries far away.

*19th C.*                               *Rev. T. Ellwood*

## HUNGER FOR HILLS

There is a hunger for hills
for the lumpy landscape
of a horizon higher than height.

A desire for creviced limestone
leached and locked
like wire teeth in a grinning skull.

A longing for cold blue skies
and a sharp wind to scatter
frosted snow on bright peaks.

A need to wonder at walls,
impossibly crawling from valleys
dipped in midday shadows.

A want of crisp ice under boot
crunched on a snowscape
empty of human form.

*1991*          *Maggie Norton*


## THE SOUND OF SNOW

The kind of silence that holds Lakeland
after heavy snowfall
is textured by the ice-melt,
punctuated by its rhythmic drips
and vainly holding in a muffled tone
the noise of wrestling captive falls.

It lies, a cold sarcophagus
for autumn's bracken, provides
a desolately resonating background
for the raven's croak.

*1990*          *Keith Ratcliffe*

## SLATE

Hacked from high hills over Honister,
Buttermere slate clothes Cumbria,
around, overhead and underfoot.

Thin, perfectly-split sheets shelter roofs,
and rough squares support stout walls,
permitting not even the faintest breath
of icy winter wind inside.
Age-old paths show little sign
of years of heavy human footstep,
and sheep find sanctuary in the lee
of the walls which wander the fells.

In town, every shop window boasts
a jagged cliff face of mottled grey-green.
German clocks and Swiss barometers,
French egg timers and Roman numerals
combine with pure English slate
to tempt tourists to buy.

Thus, without really trying,
lakes' slate
              s  p  r  e  a  d  s .

*1988*                    *Michael Park*

## NORTH

If I had not
becks for blood and
cold, green slate for
bones, day's fell would
diminish me;
dwindle me down.

Shadowed scraps of
screes, trees, deepen
in mind's corners.
Shoulders lean on
Langdale's back.
Inviolate,
I square-up to
Skiddaw's bulk,
keep sane in lake's
pooled resources.

*1989    Lydia Thomas*

## WILL THERE BE TARNS IN HEAVEN?

Will there be tarns in Heaven?
Will there be lakes as well?
Will there be waterfalls and ghylls
But peat-hags just in Hell?
Will our hereafter landscape
Resemble what we know?
Will Paradise be Borrowdale
Or Skiddaw in the snow?

And if we're posted downwards
Eternity of pain
Will all the fells be blotted out
By cold torrential rain?
Will really hardened sinners,
When life has passed away,
Drive down the M6, heading south,
For ever and a day?

*1991*                    *Glyn Matthews*

## PUTTING TO RIGHTS

That slate sky should buckle
under the huge decaying moon;   the fells
when the wind flays them, howl.
When the dead speak, the heart
should burst its capsule, shedding griefs
on good ground and stony.
But we go about our business,
measured, like gardeners, putting to rights.

*1985*                    *Meg Peacocke*

13

## WALK TO LANCASHIRE OVER SANDS

A lusty, wayward August day,
Cool, bright; capricious winds
Criss-crossed the vast seascape.
So many, all shapes, sizes, ages,
Plimsolled or barefoot, alert in anoraks,
Careless in kagoules, shorts, eager
To follow our guide over the sands.

No praise too high for Cedric Robinson,
Red-cheeked, grey-haired, merry but wise,
Mindful of quicksands and deep channels
That trap the foolish or unwary.
Far out the sea muttered and murmured,
Cheated of its prey in man's old game,
His wits against the tide.

Over this sea of sand at a great pace,
The shore dwindled behind us;
Should we ever reach home again?
Then lined up by our watchful leader
To wade thigh-deep through a channel,
Wait till he gave the word to cross.
Stragglers joined us, babes held aloft.

Onward we came, a patchwork army,
United in trust of our queen's guide.
For he was not alone; CB in hand
He talked to tractor-men far ahead
Who'd take aboard anyone who chose
The easy way, a ride home.
Determined to finish, all walked on.

Yonder we marched the rippled plain
Of treachery that long ago entrapped
Whole coaches and four, those who lost
Their deadly game to beat the tide.
Kent Bank loomed; our strength renewed,
We quickened our steps, cold but conquering.
Unforeseen black mud by the shore.

The sea reminded us the game
Was not surrendered easily.
Certificates bestowed, we cleaned ourselves;
Rode to Cartmel in search of tea.

*1992*                     *Averil King-Wilkinson*

## NIGHT SCENE, MORECAMBE BAY

The moon creeps through mother of pearl thickets,
a cosy voyeur piking on a hidden world. Velvet
blackness is broken by the line of golden prickings,
joining together remembered lines of landscape.
Now, you can count the lights at Carnforth roundabout
quivering in half a dozen miles of salty breeze,
hung over emptiness without a floor; yet intimate.
The moon, creeping behind a shelf of cloud, pushes
in on that, dropping a strobe on centre stage.
The cloud makes a lintel, proscenium arch. All
that is missing is the music. We await the entry
of the ballerina, swanning over the silver floor.

*1988*                                    *J.D. Marshall*


## PIEL CASTLE

You were never the grandest place
Just a lonely outpost, barrier
To hostile marauders.
No glorious battles were fought
Upon your ramparts,
Nor deep dark dungeons holding lost, tormented souls.

Yet, there is a minor claim to fame,
For to your doors came a Pretender.
Poor fool, he knew not what the hand of fate
Could hold in store.
How could the King allow him to succeed in his quest?

Local legend has it that you have other tales to tell
Of secret tunnels leading to a sacred vale.
Through centuries many have sought, but none can find the way.
So there you stand – a sad ruin – an interesting skyline
Crumbling, silent, bearing but one brief moment of history
That could have changed the world.

*1988*                                    *B.W. Welch*

## GEORGE FOX CROSSES THE BAY

On the beach at Bardsea, the cocklewomen
Stood watching, waiting, dry-eyed for them to drown.
Around their horses' hooves a rip-tide was racing
And swirling away the brogs of gorse

That had marked safe-passage over the sands,
So now it was too late even for them to turn.
But that spark against the dark sky,
What was it? Was it a star rising?

Was it a sign? Later they would tell
How the great God Himself had parted
The waters; how that Quaker hat of his
That stayed, God save us, undoffed

Even at Swarthmoor, had been a halo
Round his head; would bear witness
To the grit that lodged in the hard shells
Of their cockled hearts as he rode towering by.

*1982*                                     *Neil Curry*

## HARLESYDE ISLE OR CHAPEL ISLAND

A quiffed hump of trees. The grey
shape hung on silver marked with hammered
pewter. The hull floating on

> *all that marshe or comon with salte water*
> *oftentymes overflowen and overwhelmed*

with runnels and lakes, and then the creeping
torrent, obliterating toe-prints on mud
and lifting birds from lips of pool-medallions

> *leaving a certeine Isle called Harlesyde*
> *upon the sandes there called Conyshed sands.*

There is even a hump-shouldered gable, stony
against the gale that manicures the trees
leaning streamlined to the east.

> *In former times, divine service was performed*
> *at a convenient hour for such as crossed the sands.*

Thus Father West, Jesuit, seeing from comfort
the soft hand of the prior's man, cupping mercy
when the hills hung lidded over the tide's return

> *for such as crossed the sands with the*
> *morning tide. The shell of the chapel remains.*

So too the husks of a thousand traveller's tales
about dragging and humping through the channels,
and the fisherman who had a smelly hut here.

> *To have and to hold, By fealty*
> *onelie in free and common socage, and not in chief.*

Thus, a Tudor lawyer wove a net of words around
Harlesyde, to land a catch in the City, on a
May morning, five years after the Armada.

> It had been a possession of our *Soveraigne Ladie*
> *the Queen and her heires and successors.*

Now it is free for the cherishing, and the visiting,
Nobody owns it, and everybody longs for it,
and perhaps it is worth drowning for in a spring tide.

*1990*                                    *J.D. Marshall*

## A NATIVE SONG

I never go into town on the bike.
No need, you can walk where you like
in Barrow. Everything is close by.
Everyone is close by.
It's a village the size of a town.
I can't help but meet

people I know in the street:
*Remember me? I'm a friend of your mother's.*
*You can have it, I used to work with your father.*
*My youngest goes to school with your Michelle.*
*Vicky? Last I heard she wasn't very well,*
*seems happy enough though, right settled*

*apparently with this new fella,*
*tell me, did you ever –?*
I love the lilt in your accent:
it goes up at the end of a sentence,
I'd not noticed it before.
Talk to me some more.

It's a native song,
my mother tongue,
it's where I belong,
a village the size of a town
on its way down
to the size of a village.

*1990*                    *Kevin Fegan*

## THE BARROW SHIPYARD MAN

There was the Oronsay and Orcades and the Oriana too.
There was the Eva Peron for an Argentinian crew.
There was Dreadnought first and Triumph last;
There was Sheffield built, she went down fast.

There were men and steel, plates and beams
There was the Empress of Canada, built for dreams.
There was sweat and blood and the payday roll
There were the company bosses and the bloody dole.

There were smoke stacks tall and running rails bright
There were warships grey and fast, the Navy's might;
They were proud ships, beautiful, hulls sleek, bows slim
They were constructed for ever, with handcrafted trim.

But best of all there was the soft wee wife
To her and the kid, you were wedded for life.
With beer on Saturday, a booze with your mate
And holy Hell when you came home late.

*1990*                                             *M. Kavanagh*


## REG'S LAMENT
(South Lakeland Bobbin Mill)

When ah wer a lad just into mi teens
ah wer set on at t'mill one fine spring day
an ah tewk mi stand bi t'boring machine
an ah learned mi trade an ah addled mi pay...
      an t'trees in t'coppice wer young an green.

An t'hours wer long an conditions wer bad,
i summer we sweat an i winter we froze,
an t'machines raced round wi'out ony guard
an ah stood i mi place i mi working clo'es...
      an t'trees i t'coppice grew strong and tall.

An then came plastics i t'place o wood,
an t'bobbin mills shut down, one bi one,
an nobody stands wheer yance ah stood
an t'mill is silent an mi day's done...
      an t'trees in t'coppice is all cut down.

*1986*              *Kenneth Wadsworth*

## CARTMEL PRIORY

This church for centuries has watched the valley
absorbing hope and faith within its walls
built by men whose heaven waited nearer.

Over these cooled stones creeps a feeling sun,
warming from their depths an echoing
of forgotten voices, whispers of the dying,
plainsong intoned by monks, a mother's fear,
a sick child's moan, an old man's reverie.

How many prayers received expected answers,
or was it felt that praying was enough?
We who know too much yet believe too little,
can we swear we hold more of life than they
who lie in shadow near their home of prayer?

They left this church for us, a legacy
that shouts its strong assurance of a truth
even more enduring than these stones.

*1978*                              *Edward Lea*

**MEMORIAL TO THE VICARS OF URSWICK**
(for Brian Dawson)

I don't know if Matthias Forrest
Would have been taken greatly by surprise
When the news broke in Furness that his parishioners
Had sprung from apes. "Liars, drunkards, thieves,
And whoremasters following their filthy pleasures."
That was how George Fox had seen them;
And one of his brothers in Christ had been disgraced:
Scandalous in his life and negligent in his calling.

Fragments of the parish history
Survive to flesh out the names on the plaque
That Thomas Postlethwaite had put up in the chancel;
Telling us that one February
John Addison roasted a whole ox on the ice
When the Tarn had frozen over;
And that it was William Ashburner who arranged
And officiated at the cock-fights on Shrove Tuesday.

Great events of course can be worked out
From the dates: that the first awful reading
From the King James Bible would have been William Lindowe's
And it was Nicholas Marshall
Who walked in with the Book of Common Prayer, and then
Had to hold out against Cromwell.
And back, through the collapse of the monastery,
Their names go, till that last, first one, Daniel le Fleming,

Who'd have needed a smooth Norman tongue
To lick the North into holy order.
But the wonder of it all is how few of them
There were. Call them together again
And what a flimsy congregation they would seem:
Three pews would seat them all. And yet,
With time spread out like these low fells, one name's no more
Than that sudden twist in the tumbling flight of a plover.

*1985*                                          *Neil Curry*

## KNOWING YOUR PLACE

Not far along the road that crosses
Kirkby Moor, there's a stand of sycamore,
A dozen or so, their tops rounded
And buffed by the wind. Then comes the long slow
Slope of Benson's Hill on up to Horrace.

Away to the left, neglect has bewitched
A hawthorn hedge into a camel-train
Of trees climbing against the sky-line.
Horrace is a child's drawing of a house.
A right turn there takes you down to Lowick.

It's a walk I feel I have perfected.
I know the gate where the piebald ponies
Come dribbling down to have their noses rubbed;
Where brambles, as they die, take on the red
Of Indian leather, and where the Coniston Hills

Begin to unfold. One more right there
Brings you in no time to a tarn: Nut Hollow, or
Knottallow? No one seems sure. But a place
Is its own mind, and to know it truly
Is like knowing a poem: it isn't always

What the words mean that matters, but what is heard
In the silences – in the tension that exists
Between the pulls of memory and feeling.
From now on it is the sound of running water
That will be with me all the way down

To Newbiggin; to a farmhouse sheltered
By a tight fold in the hill, and built
Out of the hill. Making no claims to a view,
It is what is meant by belonging:
A collaboration and an atonement.

*1990*                                        *Neil Curry*

## MILLOM OLD QUARRY

"They dug ten streets from that there hole," he said
"Hard on five hundred houses." He nodded
Down the set of the quarry and spat in the water
Making a moorhen cock her head
As if a fish had leaped. "Half the new town
Came out of yonder – King Street, Queen Street, all
The houses round the Green as far as the slagbank,
And Market Street, too, from the Crown allotments
Up to the Station Yard." "But Market Street's
Brown freestone," I said. "Nobbut the facings;
We called them the Khaki Houses in the Boer War,
But they're Cumberland slate at the back."

I thought of those streets still bearing their royal names
Like the coat-of-arms on a child's Jubilee Mug –
Nonconformist gables sanded with sun
Or branded with burning creeper; a smoke of lilac
Between the blue roofs of closet and coal-house:
So much that woman's blood gave sense and shape to
Hacked from this dynamited combe.
The rocks cracked to the pond, and hawthorns fell
In waterfalls of blossom. Shed petals
Patterned the scum like studs on the sole of a boot,
And stiff-legged sparrows skid down screes of gravel.

I saw the town's black generations
Packed in their caves of rock, as mussel or limpet
Washed by the tidal sky; then swept, shovelled
Back in the quarry again, a landslip of lintels
Blocking the gape of the tarn.
The quick turf pushed a green tarpaulin over
All that was mortal in five thousand lives.
Nor did it seem a paradox to one
Who held quarry and query, turf and town,
In the small lock of a recording brain.

*1954*                    *Norman Nicholson*

## LIMESTONE WALLS ON BIRKRIGG

October, late afternoon; a slant
of sun through one tear
in unending cloud; a spotlight
moving on water, sand, fields,

the hill: where walls appear, white
traceries of bone
against a washed-slate
north-east sky.

Ghost walls. By light's consent
glimmering phantoms –
unfounded, as though they might not
have stood there before:

as if when light fails they might
not stand there again.

*1990*                    *Robert Drake*

## BLACK COMBE

Black Combe has no summit,
sitting in the mists like
a home-grown Ayer's Rock
covered in ferns.
Laid out like a beached whale –
skin creases steaming in
the heat of the morning;
dark fissures oozing water like wounds.
The passing train measures its length
and blue sky breaks through cloud,
giving form and shape
to its runnelled peaks –
unchanged
in ten thousand lifetimes.

*1990*                    *Michael Moon*

## WET DAY AT LEVENS HALL

Driving grey drizzle
harvested from Atlantic rollers,
obliterates cowardly sunshine.
Heavy clouds bring premature dusk
to deserted topiary garden,
where pampered and coiffured hedges
drip globules of glistening water
from each shivering twig.
Light from gift-shop doorway
spills into pathway puddles
and splashes colour across
flowers huddled in saturated beds.
Umbrella-protected visitors,
shod in multi-coloured mud,
scurry for temporary shelter
into the Elizabeth hall
and step into deep, dark shadows
(unmoved by candle-brass reflections),
slowly drip-drying in the
musky warmth of history.

*1989*                     *Michael Park*


## PLACE RHYME

Palms were round the village borne
Palms the dwellings did adorn
Crowds assembled round the thorn
On the green at Natland.

*1828*                     *T. Blezard*


*from*
## AULD STAYVLA-GAYTE FAIR

Then all were alive at the *Eagle and Child*
And at the *Duke William* mirth fairly ran wild;
No blue-coated Bobbies did then interfere;
They danced for a week at Auld Stayvla-Gayte Fair.
They drank nut-brown ale, and they drank honey-mead,
Teetotallers then had not publish'd their creed;
They drank like King Solomon to drive away care,
And keep up the spirit of Stayvla-Gayte Fair.

*1868*                     *T. Blezard*

## ST PAUL'S CHURCH, RUSLAND

Rock upon its rocky mound
Shaped stone that shapes the church
Against the background of rising trees.
The wind stirs the trees upon the hills
But the valley holds its breath
Quietly, as it holds the church.

The organ menders arrived
By the gate we entered.
With one from the church to whom I spoke,
Who carried in his eyes the valley's quiet,
Wore calmness like a cloak
And knew the rock within the ground.

And yet his words, like spits of wind
Where stone walls have crumbled,
Touching the unwary traveller,
Make him aware of slow time's changes.
The sure defences gone.
Cold breath of uncertainty.

The church is built on rock.
Guarded all round with hills and woods.
But I felt the cold whispers of winds
Touch the skin of my mind,
And knew rocks were fractured.

The peaceful dead outnumber all the living parish
In your churchyard. Amongst so many lost and unknown names
Lies one, much known. And I hear the sound of children's voices
Rising, from the lake beyond the hills, and from another age
That cradled the church more surely than its rock and valley.

Arthur Ransome, in your stony grave
Cannot your ghost spin out another yarn,
Call other days and, in magic on the lake, steer
Much brighter boats than the cabin cruisers now on Windermere.

*1980*                                              *W.A. Mellors*

## LOW LUDDERBURN

I climbed up Ludderburn Hill today
Past Hartbarrow farm where kittens play
In the September sun.
Climbing the hill I know so well
To meet the road to Cartmel Fell
Past coppice woods,
And bungalows built into the hill
But there's a lonely wildness still
About this place.

And to the right the hills, the views,
Low Ludderburn, its two great yews
Stand sentinels in green,
Where owls at night sang down their note
Down to the barn where Arthur wrote
Of Swallows on the lake.

*1990*                              *George Wray*


## SWALLOW SUMMER

Standing alone at the lakeside I sense
this breeze that ruffles wavelets catching my hair,
feel I am Swallow bound.
I share thrill of turning into each tack,
flag flutter, words carried away
on light current. I am an island child;
spring water, fire and fish are all I need.
My shelter is a blanket under stars,
my few companions all humanity.
My dark side is adventure,
skulls and charcoal, still black water.

Standing alone at the lakeside I sense
fusion of dusty rooms and dusty books
with childhood – theirs and mine – both gilded,
both petrified. I walk away; grow up;
know that the Swallow's crew
treads in my shadow and runs on ahead.

*1991*                              *Alison Chisholm*

**RUSKIN'S TREES**

Thin Coniston water,
flat as the hills are steep;
sheep stuck on impossible slopes
stop pulling grass to gaze
as Bluebird plumes
somersaulting through
her first dash backwash –
the bang lifts waterbirds
and sprays with magic
a hero's disappearance.

Across the lake
two ghosts, dissimilar
but twinned by failure, stare
from a Brantwood window
as first faint ripples lap
the stones – and Campbell's teddy,
Waterspeed World Champion Bear,
bobs among the fuel and glassy fish...
And Ruskin's trees point frozen
tips towards an angel-laden sky.

*1990*                    *David Phillips*


**THE OLD MAN OF CONISTON**

Watch the mountain shifting with the hour,
emerging from the mist leaning to view
its yawning face within the lake below,
disdainfully turning, then greyly scowling –
as if resentful it cannot scatter
clouds gathering on its brow –
too briefly feeling a moment's warmth
as its face lights up after rain.
A tamed yet tethered beast it merely waits
while winds run shuffling down the lake –
each gust destroying reflections –
shouldered a future uncertain as
weather.  Raised when man slept unaware,
it hangs in time like one more spore of dust.

*1980*                    *Edward Lea*

## WHITE TRAINS LOG

*March.* Woke
shaking from dreams
lay for a long time
while the train
grumbled away
through the town.

*April.* They
come hourly
through darkness
concealing
black suns radiant
on yellow skies.

*June.* Night
too short and
threadbare now
to hide
the poisoned cups
they send.

*1990*

*September.* More
often than hours
the trembling
down deep
hugging myself
for comfort.

*October.* Woke
to silence
five nights
and no trains
this, this
worst of all.

*Robert Drake*


## GREY CROFT

Fire generated them
from deep within
the core of a volcano.
Millenniums passed them by;
then they were gathered up –
together they made this a place of power;
and once within the centre of their ring
burnt funeral fires, that scorched off human skin.
they are still there – each seems to wait and watch
remembering some purpose long eclipsed.
Some look towards the sea,
some turn to face inland –
to Sellafield,
less than a mile away –

*1991*                                        *Fiona Walker*

## SEASCALE AND WINDSCALE

Seascale.  Once a small resort
Famous for golf and a girl's school
A straggle of houses, a village shop,
Children's chatter on the beach.
Summer-time, in train loads,
Sunday schools arrived
In shouting hordes The Sea!  The Sea!
Mothers primly withdrew
Their superior brats
From the crowded shore.

Now, boxes of dwellings
An annexe for Windscale
The giant greedy for water
Devourer of landscape,
Whose scientists
Try to reassure us.

I walk the deserted shore,
Thinking of times past,
The ancient cross
Still stands at Gosforth,
Cows munch placidly
In nearby fields.  Saddened,
I watch the setting sun
Redden a suspect sea.

*1981*                    *Kate Lindsay*

## ON THE BEACH

Earth rock sand –
our beginning,
being;
thence flora,
fauna,
humankind.

Microscopic granite sparks,
grains of splintered flint,
granulated sandstone,
crystallized cliff-specks,
myriad molecules
of powdered pebble,
fawn, ochre, russet,
bluish, seaweed tinted,
minute mineral life-seeds,
many-faceted,
pin-point mirrored,
mass of ground stone atoms
all crushed coalesced
into this stretch
of smooth shining shore,
so suavely deceptive,
that has in store
for children paddling,
digging in the sky-wet sand
something unlooked for:
beach particles filmed around,
infused invisibly
tainted with unexpected
geiger-crackling nuclear venom.

The children's spades
constructing fairy castles
unearth concealed micro-germs,
release death-rays.
In such a place
people playing at the sea's edge
will probably be poisoned,
slowly killed.

*1983*        *Pat Arrowsmith*

## CUMBRIAN VILLAGE
### (Staveley-in-Kendal)

It may be there are wayside halts
more intimate than this:
hamlets where the houses rest
in tempered stone more equably
where the chestnuts lift,
the lilacs drift,
diviner pinnacles;
the sun-stropped becks have braver edge,
the sedges greener gallantry.

It may be this is one moment
patterned universally;
nor this the only village sacred
to the wild elegance of swifts.
But here, within a homefront air
so visibly, explicitly endowed,
all other vistas seem extravagantly bodiless;
mere lantern magic, immaterial.

*1953*                    *Geoffrey Holloway*

*from*
## FROST AT MIDNIGHT

My babe so beautiful!  it thrills my heart
With tender gladness, thus to look at thee,
And think that thou shalt learn far other lore
And in far other scenes!  For I was reared
In the great city, pent 'mid cloisters dun,
And saw naught lovely but the sky and stars.
But *thou*, my babe!  shalt wander like a breeze
By lakes and sandy shores, beneath the crags
Of ancient mountain, and beneath the clouds...
Therefore all seasons shall be sweet to thee...

*1798*             *Samuel Taylor Coleridge*

## WATER SKIER: WINDERMERE

From the hothouse coach, through sweat-dazzled spectacles,
caught up and moving with him we admire
how gloriously, audaciously he goes;
the ice-cold brilliance of a charioteer
with a shear-edge of incontestable modernity;
leaving it all behind him, weaving
through the flak of sunbursts, the shock of buoys –
his wake decisive as a vapour trail,
frost-vehement, assured.

Moving with him, managing for once
the reins of destiny in fast, dramatic hands,
we also touch fulfilment;  through the glass
of lustrous alchemistic envy turn
the dross to dreams, to a perspective where
the future is the sun's, iridescent, easy;
the spills spray out in laughter, and the past
across the classic fiord leans serenely irreproachable:
the wing of a lectern eagle, brazen gold.

*1954*                           *Geoffrey Holloway*


## LOOKING ACROSS THE LAKE FROM STORRS

It rains, rains, the lake and sky are one,
No line to mark where one begins or ends
The waves roll on, roll on,
The steamer, awnings dripping, to Lakeside wends
Through the squall, then it has gone.

Storrs Temple my refuge from the rain,
Where damp poets may stand sentinel for half a day,
And try in vain, in vain,
To look ahead and penetrate the grey,
Glimpse the vision and hope it will remain.

*1984*                           *George Wray*

## BEATRIX POTTER, MRS HEELIS & HILL TOP FARM

She was throughout her life a very private
person, projecting shyness
through years of unexpected reputation:
poet in paint with gifts of observation
Millais commended, whether drawing fungi,
rabbits or mice:  locked within herself
in a deep privacy few penetrated.

Hill Top at Sawrey saw the consummation
of quiet girlhood dreams and secret talents.
Here she was free to be her truest self
among the gentle folded hills, the lanes
winding round Esthwaite's cottages and farms;
and working beside practical rural folk
on practical rural matters that she loved
her life unfolded like a happy fiction
of homespun magic and simplicity.

Although she's gone her work lives on untouched
by time or fashion;  early nursery loves
transmuted into art, and she'd not change
one Hill Top item;  not a doll or dress
of her dear treasure house shall be disturbed.
The years ahead must all be as before.
And her beloved landscape lives on too
unchanged through forty years – Esthwaite still
the loveliest most intimate of lakes,
a placid sheet of water softly etched
against a distant mountain view and washed
in quiet greens and blues of summer skies
and mist of rainy April afternoons,
where between Jemima's twiggy wood
and Pigling's road that led to Market Town
in peaceful Sawrey fields her dust is scattered,
still intimate with all she loved in life.

*1985*                    *John Barron Mays*

## LAST NIGHT IN CUMBRIA
(to Beatrix Potter)

From your bed
you see white gulls flatter
the chalk grey sky.
You have written your last letter to the shepherd.
He was born here, he knows
every sheep has its own face,
every hill its own path.
It took you half a life-time to put on
the old rough overcoat of earth, to go
eccentric and behatted
like the Cumbrian sun.

When you were a child
freedom was a rabbit behind bars,
a fox you disembowelled.
Upstairs you made little books,
a sign post to fame and fortune.
You were never fooled:
Your business was always close at hand.
Tonight when your world is tied to the sun's mast
it is the shepherd you have in mind,
his winter lambs.

*1991*                          *Susan Skinner*

## BRAYSTONES

It was the hermit-crab
   started the fashion
   with an instinct grave as thought, needing
   a shield for nakedness.
Seafarers took it up
   in ignorance, when the storm
   had heaved them back on shore, and tossed
   their emptied shells
   of boats behind them;
   houses for homeless creatures.

Piece by piece
   additions came;  the crab
   placed his anemone
   as camouflage, and inadvertently
   made beauty.
Through the roof-ridge keel
   a chimney pokes;  about the door
   finest of stones define a private place,
   and Pegotty's at home
   with curtains.

This century's traveller
   looks down from the Coastal Line
   and notes the carriage roof
   making the arching spine
   of another sea-edge home.
Another make-do man
   has crabwise added
   extensions to his life;
an extra hearth-place needed,
   he has leaned
   to front and rear new rooms,
   his proof and claim
   against the surge beating his shingle bounds.
He's anchored here
   his raft of concrete.
   What he needs
   of food and folk will surely come his way.
The rest
   will pass,
   on tide or train.

*1988*                          *Frances Marshall*

## TILBERTHWAITE

That afternoon we went to Tilberthwaite,
And stood on the slate-sliced bridge
Above the beck;
I thought what I'd remember
Would be brown water,
The busyness of it,
The going-somewhere water
Flowing like warm oil,
But instead it was a boy,
Crouched on the edge of my vision,
At the stony edge of the beck,
So much at one with sky and water,
Merging into it,
There and not there,
Forever having been there,
That the landscape seemed to have
Folded him like a mountain catchfly
into itself.

*1985*          *Marie Stewart*




## BRIDGE HOUSE, AMBLESIDE

On the steps,
mother and two children smile,
while father points a camera:
click!
This slate stack
straddling Stock Ghyll
appears in photo albums
from Jarrow to Japan.
A former pigeon loft,
counting house,
cobblers,
once, its two tiny rooms
housed a family of six.

Now, pilgrims pack this folly
relic of two centuries
to learn the paths of Loughrigg.

*1991*          *Pat Livingston*

## THE GRAVEDIGGER'S GUIDE TO SURREALISM

Watchful as carrion crows we loitered
among yew-trees: Jack Haddow the sexton,
pensioned-off by angina; and the apprentice
gravedigger, with mud-stained boots and jeans;
while the black flock lodged its long box
of grief in my first grave.

Jack murmured cautionary tales: of graves
too short or narrow for their cargo; of stones
dislodged that rolled down, jamming wood to soil
until the poor dead hung in mid-air; of wet holes
filling so fast that coffins floated
slowly back up to the living...

and a sexton's horror-stories: of side-walls
that fell and spilled the contents
of an old grave into the new; the dangers
of re-opening, an accidental foot thrust
through a soft coffin-lid into the grey
soup of a dead husband or wife.

The straggle of hunched mourners
wound through the churchyard; we crept out
from hiding. Among the graves Jack stopped
by a squat headstone. "Empty, that one.
He was some kind of artist, made pictures
from rubbish – bus-tickets and bike-wheels.

Ever heard of him?" I read the name:
KURT SCHWITTERS, but knew nothing then
of our century's mundane debris moulded
in years of sculpted plaster on the wall
of a stone-built barn, surely
as flesh melds with subsoil.

"He died at Ambleside, but
later they dug him up and took him
home to Germany. So
it's empty" Jack said over his shoulder,
weaving among leaning grey stones
towards the waiting grave.

*1991*                    *Robert Drake*

## VIKING DIG: KENTMERE

Clouds, indigo whales,
lurch towards the horizon.

The wind practises snow topiary;
grim hunchbacks drip slowly
where gateways have been cleared.

Sheep lick the rolling tops
of giant plastic tubs.
Threads of molasses
glint from their gums.

The old reservoir
fills with snow streams.
A matted ewe lies
near the edge,
skull and pelvis
excavated.

The fellside caravan
that housed the dig
– a summer shieling
near fresh pasture –
is shards of aluminium
against a drystone wall

a smashed sofa
half-buried in snow,
black bin liners
full of jumbled finds –

a smudged tag stuck in ice.

*1985*          *Patricia Pogson*

## THE LAMBS OF GRASMERE

The upland flocks grew starved and thinned:
    Their shepherds scarce could feed the lambs
Whose milkless mothers butted them,
    Or who were orphaned of their dams.
The lambs athirst for mother's milk
    Filled all the place with piteous sounds:
Their mother's bones made white for miles
    The pastureless wet pasture grounds.

Day after day, night after night,
    From lamb to lamb the shepherds went,
With teapots for the bleating mouths,
    Instead of nature's nourishment.
The little shivering gaping things
    Soon knew the step that brought them aid,
And fondled the protecting hand,
    And rubbed it with a woolly head.

Then, as the days waxed on to weeks,
    It was a pretty sight to see
These lambs with frisky heads and tails
    Skipping and leaping on the lea,
Bleating in tender trustful tones,
    Resting on rocky crag or mound
And following the beloved feet
    That once had sought for them and found.

These very shepherds of their flocks,
    These loving lambs so meek to please,
Are worthy of recording words
    And honour in their due degrees;
So might I live a hundred years,
    And roam from strand to foreign strand,
Yet not forget this flooded spring
    And scarce-saved lambs of Westmoreland.

*1860*                         *Christina Rossetti*

## WORDSWORTH'S UMBRELLA

A parasol for the rain, large enough to accommodate
wet friends – De Quincey, Southey – or the household
women.  Often it sheltered Dorothy as they walked
in lanes and fields of seeping hues:
the hilltops came and went under cloud,
water feeding the lakes, the lakes the land.

Lichen-coloured now, it's out of the damp,
a museum companion to the cloak and hat;
nearby, another record of lakeland days –
Coleridge's "Ode to the Rain", in notebook hand.

I emerge again into insistent drizzle,
anoraked, watching the walkers in kagoules,
harsh colours against the subtle Grasmere greens.
That verdigree umbrella, giant fungus, blended
far better with this scene, aesthetic adjunct
to arthritic trees.  I sneeze, reminded of Dorothy's
"*Wm. slept ill.  A soaking all-day rain*";
of William's "*The rain came heavily and fell in floods*";
and how she dried his hair before the peat fire
steadily glowing, the heart of their house place.
So powerful the link, the lakes seem theirs.

It recalls Ambleside, a honeymoon:
the future seemed as vast as Windermere
though misty at the edge;
in happy student poverty we walked
great lengths, wet fells, close under his umbrella –
our sole house place in those first days.
Since then, showers, monsoons:
the lakes absorb them and remain unchanged.
Returning now, I celebrate to find
an ancient umbrella and the same fine rain.

*1986*                                    *Gladys Mary Coles*

## DOROTHY WORDSWORTH WAKES AT ALLAN BANK

So she woke here, even as I wake here,
And saw, as I do, from her quiet bed,
The great mountain's shoulder, the deep cleft,
Where Michael worked at his unfinished fold.
Dorothy woke here in the early morning,
To her world of mountain and stream, which, long familiar,
Yet gave her each new day its cool grave secrets,
In essential loveliness, as one might lay
In the hand of a tried friend some intimate token.
She woke to hear the patter of running feet,
To watch, with virginal affectionate glamour,
William's wild loving brood of little children.
She woke to her steady certainty of faith
In William's genius. If her heart could question
Whether any days could be like those first days
With him, she quietly reassured herself
That he was great, and she had nourished him,
Could nourish him yet, and so fulfil herself,
And bring his thoughts to birth. She woke to share
With shy Mary, a hundred household cares,
Putting out all the rareness of her spirit
Into some simple duty, and interlacing
Plain work with delicate gold of new perceptions,
Gathered within, without, from field or book.
She woke to steady herself against a hurt
So deep she could no longer weep for it;
To see the death in life of the man she loved,
As he had foretold it so sharply and pitifully
In the poems which he would never write any more.
'Tis this that made her womanhood more frail,
That checks the flow of the sap: and yet I see her
Bravely vigorous in spirit and body,
With quick chaste movements, dressing herself demurely,
With half her mind at work out of the window,
She who never spoke of the colour or shape
Of any dress she wore, being more concerned
With the birch tree's habit, or the mountain's cloak,
William's genius unfaltering here, was sure
When he saw her kin to the natural wild things,
The lover and  beloved of the sheltered valley,
And high enfolding hills.

*1930*                                    *Margaret Cropper*

## WORDWORTH'S OLD AGE

Sunlight once played upon the granite ledges
Now shadowed by austerity of mind;
And from the place where primroses have rested
The warm earth has declined.
Cold is the rock face, moss and lichen banished
To green forgotten springs locked deep below
A frozen crust; the celandine has vanished.
Where star and violet shone now falls the snow.

You, the river brimmed with life reflecting
Forms and colours we could not perceive
Until you shone the mirror through our blindness,
Are now a dry bed where the willows grieve.

Can old age answer for a poet's dying?
(Those bony fingers pinch a shrinking flame.)
Or was it passion cold upon the anvil
That failed your sensual heart till no spark came
To startle innate iron with sudden glory
Transcending vulgar metal? Was it shame
Or sanctioned love that tamed your blue-hawk spirit,
Drugging the Muse with kindness and with calm,
And dropped domestic oil on seething torrents
To sooth such ecstasy with deadly balm?

You who wrote your name in rock and rainbow
And sang of summits till you dwarfed the earth,
Are now tight-lipped, ungiving as the gritstone
Lodge for the bones where once a bird had birth.
When the heart is out no hearth-fire warms the poet;
To find a spark his will must strike on stone.
But stone is hostile to a tired spirit –
The poet is dead: a man lives on alone.

*1954*                           *Phoebe Hesketh*


*from*
## MEMORIAL VERSES

Keep fresh the grass upon his grave,
O Rotha, with thy living wave!
Sing him thy best! for few or none
Hears thy voice right, now he is gone.

*1853*            *Matthew Arnold*

43

## WILLIAM WORDSWORTH

No room for mourning:  he's gone out
Into the noisy glen, or stands between the stones
Of a gaunt ridge, or you'll hear his shout
Rolling among the screes, he being a boy again.
He'll never fail nor die
And if they laid his bones
In the wet vaults or iron sarcophagi
Of fame, he'd rise at the first summer rain
And stride across the hills to seek
His rest among the broken lands and clouds.
He was a stormy day, a granite peak
Spearing the sky;  and look, about its base
Words flower like crocuses in the hanging woods,
Blank though the dalehead and the bony face.

*1941*                                    *Sidney Keyes*


## EXQUISITE SISTER

"More than half a poet", she said,
close-knit with William.  In his work
her phrases shine – that stunted thorn,
the moon among a black-blue vault,
a whirl-blast from behind the hill,
the tossing, reeling daffodil,
a butterfly, the beggar seen in May.

Recording all, the walks, the Lakeland scene,
the talks, she sees herself
guardian, provider of a frame
to nurture genius.  The homely images
slip from her pen – William sleeps well,
sleeps badly, William sat
"feasting with silence," – leaves his broth

untouched, sets off with John,
cold pork in pocket, fishes in the lake.
Her Journals sparkle, bring them both to life.
She mends old clothes, spreads linen, hoes the peas,
but never views herself in a true light.
Writer, observer, fitly linked with those
whose pen illuminates, a poet in prose.

*1988*                                    *M.A.B. Jones*

## DE QUINCEY

Twice he approached but could not face
acquaintance with his idol.  Reaching the lake
at Coniston, once walking on
to where the gorge of Hammerscar
opened the Grasmere view, he saw
the valley clear.  Below, feathered to the edge
with wildflower, fern,
water that stretched to fields – and there
two bowshots off, Dove Cottage shone.
Yet still he shrank, retreated
as a shamed and guilty one.

Diffidence natural perhaps – strangers
before a man to whom
he was but name.  A want of confidence:
youth the enthusiast
stumbling upon the rocklike skill of age.
Or was it more – the fear we share
losing illusion when we find
that gods and idols have their feet of clay.

Whatever reason, there
flight, fate, wife, future lay.

*1988*                          *M.A.B. Jones*

## GRASMERE SPORTS

In a green arena,
Wrestlers, in bright trunks,
Ply an ancient sport.
Once, wrestling was a sport for Kings.
A local lad threw King Edward's champion
And claimed he ate for breakfast
Porridge, with cream
A mouse could walk on.

Next came the Fell races.
Lean men trot off
A thousand feet or more,
And are back in fifteen minutes
To brass bands, cheerful crowds.

Best of all, the hounds, tails quivering,
Tense as their owners
Race out of sight,
Pads barely touching the ground;
High on the fell
We see them strung out.

Owners roar as the first is sighted.
Not just the winners are praised.
A blissful sport,
With nothing killed
For our delight.

*1990*            *Kate Lindsay*

## THE SNOW MIRACLE
### A Legend of Saint Bees

Go, Lady, ask Lord Lucy of his grace
To grant us land, so did Saint Bega say,
Where we may rear a house to watch and pray:
The storm that flung us to the landing-place
Robbed us of all. Lord Lucy from the chase
Came laughing home: Good dame, I answer, Nay,
Yet promise all on next Midsummer day
Is white with snow to mend the stranger's case.
God hath His book, St. Bega's prayer is won,
Vows made in haste are vows eternally:
There came the hallow-eve of Great Saint John,
Forth looked the young moon from a sultry sky;
But ere the night to Midsummer had gone,
Beneath the snow three miles of seaboard lie.

*1887*                    *H.D. Rawnsley*

## ST BEES HEAD

The start of the journey.
Up high to the brow,
Climbing his thick shoulder
To the harsh red rock face,
Weathered ruddy by the North.
It is bearded by kind heathers
Tipped grey as in old age.

His sunken chin lazes in the
Shallows as he stares out to sea,
And daily he is more jagged
As particles flake and desert him.
So the giant's features become
More defined, severe
With the passing of seasons.
So his responsibility grows
With fame, as the crowds swell,
Pulsing through St Bees
On the start of their journey.

*1991*          *Martyn Astley*

## CLEATOR MOOR

From one shaft at Cleator Moor
They mined for coal and iron ore.
This harvest below ground could show
Black and red currants on one tree.

In furnaces they burnt the coal,
The ore they smelted into steel,
And railway lines from end to end
Corseted the bulging land.

Pylons sprouted on the fells,
Stakes were driven in like nails,
And the ploughed fields of Devonshire
Were sliced with the steel of Cleator Moor.

The land waxed fat and greedy too,
It would not share the fruits it grew,
And coal and ore, as sloe and plum,
Lay black and red for jamming time.

The pylons rusted on the fells,
The gutters leaked beside the walls
The women searched the ebb-tide tracks
For knobs of coal and broken sticks.

But now the pits are wick with men,
Digging like dogs dig for a bone:
For food and life *we* dig the earth –
In Cleator Moor they dig for death.

Every waggon of cold coal
Is fire to drive a turbine wheel;
Every knuckle of soft ore
A bullet in a soldier's ear.

The miner at the rockface stands,
With his segged and bleeding hands
Heaps on his head the fiery coal
And feels the iron in his soul.

*1954*            *Norman Nicholson*

## A MEMORY OF JONATHAN SWIFT

Just a dozen yards
from the old *Red Flag*
a mere stone's throw from where Dean Swift was nursed as a child
is a Brobdignagian monster of a candlestick.
Eighty feet of Georgian granite
whose shadow daily moves across the beachscape
where Swift saw Lilliputian figures
busying themselves on the harbourside
a hundred feet below.

Coincidence, yes, certainly;
strange how a flue for a coalmine,
a safety valve for methane gas
should have such a Swiftian feel to it
– or am I just a dreamer?

*1991*                    *Michael Moon*


## SIGNING NOW FOR DEMERARA

Circumscribed iron stobs:
twentytwo in number –
sewn like Dragon's teeth,
pick out the point of the compass
at Whitehaven's *Green Market.*
Where, once, seafaring men were hired
and tall tales told;
where skills in splicing rope
carried more weight than facial scars
or a full complement of fingers.
Here in days of old
voyage deals were struck
over a firm handshake and piece of bitten gold.
Where pigtails and rum-soaked, buckled shoes
brought home the recent foreign news.
And memories of this small piece of ground
fluted iron stobs, a lock-up and a lamp
were taken to many a sailor's grave.

*1991*                    *Michael Moon*

*from*
## LINES ON THE WRESTLING AT WHITEHAVEN

Descend now, ye gods, from Olympus on high,
To view Cumbria's sons, – and get your steam up and fly;
Amongst you there's fine-looking fellows and clever,
But mortals like these did your godships see ever?

Behold but Banks Bowe! saw you ere aught like him?
Or Chapman's full muscle, fine symmetry, limb?
Or Brunskill, a model for sculptors to study,
Round face, fair mustachios, countenance ruddy?

Now the wrestling's begun, so your godships goodbye,
You may just soar about 'twixt the earth and the sky,
To observe how the heroes cross-buttock, hype, heel,
And at home o'er your nectar these wonders reveal.

First Swat, alias Adam Parke, lad of spring steel,
Like a basket-rod tough, thou turn'st like an eel;
Though strength overwhelm'd thee, thy glory shalt shine,
And Bards round thy temples fame's laurels entwine.

With laughter all hail'd thee, good Dominie Graham,
Thy parson-like look and thy iron-rod frame,
But soon chang'd was laughter to boundless applause:
Thou grass'd thy men cleanly 'midst deaf'ning huzzas.

William Bateman, the vet'ran, of thee next I sing,
A braver old wrestler ne'er entered a ring;
Thy science and energy seem undecayed,
And many a hero thou prostrate has laid.

The triumphs of Chapman my song ne'er can tell,
Or how Brunskill brave like the forest oak fell;
How Graham, with black coat on, still gallantly won,
Till forc'd to submit to the great Tomlinson.

I would dwell on your merits till spring flowers bloom,
Yes, delighted continue till time seal'd my doom;
Exhorting each Bard and each votary of mirth,
To carol your praises in sky and on earth.

*1838*                                      *John Hardie*

## ON WANSFELL

I belong nowhere
and to no one
if not to the mountain I lie upon,
the ash tree I lie under
whose leaves' silent music stays
uprising and returning.

Hours, days
are sanded away in the sound
of a harvester –
by this and a leaf-muffled stream
and the wasp-thin hum of a plane,
are all things bound.

*1986*                    *Phoebe Hesketh*




*from*
## STANZAS

Dread cliff of Baruth! *that* wild wish may sleep,
Bold as if men and creatures of the Deep
Breathed the same element; too many wrecks
Have struck thy sides, too many ghastly decks
Hast thou looked down upon, that such a thought
Should here be welcome, and in verse enwrought:
With thy stern aspect better far agrees
Utterance of thanks that we have passed with ease
As millions thus shall do, the Headlands of St. Bees.

*1833*                    *William Wordsworth*

## INVASION FAIRFIELD, 2000 BC

Neolithic man first roamed your slopes,
His blood maybe it was that stained
The sundew red
With glacial stones from Brathay's bed
The Romans built Galava in your shade.
    Came Angli with their ox-drawn plough,
Tilling land made fertile by your becks.
    Next raiding Viking
Bringing crafts and skills,
Working iron for their swords
Adding Scandinavian words –
Skali, gafl, knutr, hyjartar, gringler, ghyll.
    Then the conquest of the Norman
With his monast'ry and Pele;
Hamlets growing, commerce flowing
Through his industry and zeal.
Yet the border still unsettled
As attacking Scots converge –
To waste Furness, ravage homesteads,
Over Solway Bay they surge.
    Now invasion comes by highway
More insidious malaise,
Where pack-horses once would stumble
Juggernauts to Windscale rumble
Changing gear on Dunmail Raise.
    In the year AD two thousand
Will the Scandale Beck run clear,
No acid rain to scorch your turf,
No nuclear waste to foul the air?
    An encroachment brings new hazards
You assimilate, condone;
Tonight as "The Merry Dancers" glow
You assume Aurora's crown.
    Heron Pike, Great Rigg and Hart Crag
Quarter your heraldic shield,
Through the troubled tide of ages
Your escutcheons blaze FAIR FIELD.

*1981*                    *Sheona Lodge*

## NAMING HILLS

All afternoon
I sat on rocks watching the fells
massing on skyline –
a great herd of hills,
heaving huge arcs and flanks,
rounded heads and butting crags,
horning the clouds.

Like animals,
they kept their privacy,
held their own nature,
were just what they were,
tossed sun from steaming scarps,
mottled in shade,

and though
like animals,
we gave them names,
they did not know
or care, or feel in their
vast unconcern,
that we had named them
Bow Fell or Wetherlam,
Pike of Stickle, Crinkle or Scafell.

They did not speak our tongue,
had names
we did not choose,
had their own slow secret
not for me to tell.

*1980*          *Margaret Pain*


## COUNTING SHEEP NEAR SEATOLLER

Leaping
from bank to road,
the ewe halts
a flock of cars.
Stationary,
she turns
to scrutinise the leader
daring it to move,
before she scurries on
to greener grass.

*1991*          *Pat Livingston*

## SHEEP

They dot the moor like mice on a green mat.
Nearer, they have their heads down to the
board, nodding to cues of food.

Shorn, their ribs hang from hammocky
spines, a grey spareness picked
by the canines of the high wind.

They toddle pert-footed up the puckered
slope, not noticing the broken rocks,
and letting human shapes pass keyhole eyes.

Jaws cranking, they reflect the robbers
who wear sacks and coils of wool round
white necks tortoising from anoraks –

and prepare – to turn powder-shot of
snow from the winter's thatch of fleece,
oblivious to the stiffened human lost.

*1989*                           *J.D. Marshall*


## JENNY'S FARM

There is a farm on green Longsleddale flank,
With broken walls and vestiges of roof
And outbuildings once stout and warm with life,
But now cold refuge for the rambling fox.
The last grim man to farm this sloping land
Saw two sons march to die in Flanders mud:
His daughter's beau returned, but two years on,
While still unwed, fell climbing Pillar Rock.
So Jenny lived alone when Father died,
Contemptuous of proposals and all help,
Sold half the land and stock and barred the gate:
As years went by, less and less often seen
In wary passage to the tongue-tied store.
She died, threescore and ten, gaunt friendless maid;
Then wind and rain and sleet, and boisterous youths
Dislodged the slates and buffeted the walls,
And drove away all human memories,
No ghost walks here: sometimes on the roof,
Above the gaping kitchen of the house,
A little owl keeps stern offended watch.

*1990*                           *Glyn Matthews*

**BORROWDALE IN A SHOWER**
(from *Iteriad*)

The morning appeared with a great face of doubt,
Or to make us keep in, or to let us go out;
And at the first opening of joy-bringing dawn
Dark cloaks of thick cloud round the mountain were drawn.
We look out of window, – call guides after guides, –
Demand whether rain or fair weather betides.
The first puts his thumb on one side of his nose,
And looks up to the smoke, to see how the wind blows;
Then pronounces it after a great deal of puffing,
"A vara bad dai! Why, you couldn't see nothing!"
The next, – "Whai, ye sees, sir, I'se can't hardly say;
Boot I'se think that it may be a middlin' fair day."
Another, – "For Skudda this never will do,
But I think's it prove fine, though not fit for a view:
And so if you liked it, a trip you might take
By Borrowdale, down into Boothermere lake."

*1830*                                    *John Ruskin (aged 11)*

*from*
**THE BROTHERS**

"These Tourists, heaven preserve us! needs must live
A profitable life: some glance along,
Rapid and gay, as if the earth were air,
And they were butterflies to wheel about
Long as the summer lasted: some, as wise,
Perched on the forehead of a jutting crag,
Pencil in hand and book upon knee,
Will look and scribble, scribble on and look,
Until a man might travel twelve stout miles
Or reap an acre of his neighbour's corn."

*1800*                                    *William Wordsworth*

## THORN HOUSE, LOWER HARTSOP
(for Ed and Kate Hill)

Watcher approach the house and see its gable
pointing up Gray Crag three hundred years

Pass by between Mireside Burfitt and Pingle fields
to look along the glen to Threshwaite Mouth

Turn the eye to Hartsop Dod and watch a single runner
passing out of sight towards the peak

and lingering fear your loneliness possessed
by a spirit of those who shepherded across these fells

themselves possessed by nature's urgency
pairing to propagate their own rare breed

piling their lives like stones on history
giving the hillside and the becks their names

Come back and stand beneath this gallery
much photographed where wool was spun

watch and assume the essences perhaps
of Quaker silences the house once held

A ram's skull at the door images some pagan deity
whose influence is still not far removed

and standing over it the rusting iron cross confirms
a watcher's closeness to the mystery of earth.

*1991*                                    *Alan Gaunt*

## THE MAID OF BUTTERMERE
(from *The Prelude*)

I mean O distant Friend!  a story drawn
From our own ground – the Maid of Buttermere, –
And how, unfaithful to a virtuous wife
Deserted and deceived, the Spoiler came
And wooed the artless daughter of the hills,
And wedded her, in cruel mockery
Of love and marriage bonds.  These words to thee
Must needs bring back the moment when we first,
Ere the broad world rang with the maiden's name,
Beheld her serving at the cottage inn;
Both stricken, as she entered or withdrew,
With admiration of her modest mien
And carriage, marked by unexampled grace.
We since that time not unfamiliarly
Have seen her, – her discretion have observed,
Her just opinions, delicate reserve,
Her patience, and humility of mind
Unspoiled by commendation and the excess
Of public notice – an offensive light
To a meek spirit suffering inwardly.

From this memorial tribute to my theme
I was returning, when, with sundry forms
Commingled – shapes which met me in the way
That we must tread – thy image rose again,
Maiden of Buttermere!  She lives in peace
Upon the spot where she was born and reared;
Without contamination doth she live
In quietness, without anxiety:
Beside the mountain-chapel, sleeps in earth
Her new-born infant, fearless as a lamb
That, thither driven from some unsheltered place
Rests underneath the little rock-like pile
When storms are raging...

*1805*                           *William Wordsworth*

## SCARTH GAP, BUTTERMERE

There is no need to describe the track;  a pencil
Drawn diagonally across a slate
Would be more precise than words.  Stone walls
Lay ladders of grey against the green;  the green
Glissades into the lake.
This pass is known, defined and understood
Not by the eyes but by the feet,
The feet of men and sheep that tread it;  the young
Teacher from Cleator Moor, pushing a bike
With a burnish of poetry on the rims;
The girl who is soon to bear a foreigner's child;
The lad who leaves the pit shafts of the Solway
To grope for a brighter fire than coal.
These, in the clang and shuffle of the world,
Are shunted along strange, disordered rails,
To crash on viaducts or into buffers
Or bide in sidings where nightshade trails on the lines.
That world they rejected once, perhaps once only,
And scrambled up the screes of the slithering moment
To seek a combe unquarried yet by change,
Where memory, returning with the wheatear,
Could find the name scratched on the same stone,
Therefore to them this dale, this pass,
This double queue of hills, High Stile and Mellbreak,
Robinson, Grassmoor and Hobcarton Fell,
(Themselves the wrack and backwash
Of the geological tides) seem now
More lasting memorial than the rubble of cities –
A track that the wild herdwicks still will tread
Long years after the makers of tracks are dead.

*1954*                                    *Norman Nicholson*

## A6: SHAP FELL, 1952

Keep your eyes off the road, gut and glory
of the commerce drive gouging desperately through,
its only arbiters quick profits, time.

Keep your eyes off the means, moaning trucks
with humpbacks and heavy straps,
their noses to a granite grindstone.

Off the crews, the regulars: jerkined toughs,
the smoke of Woodbines like a pickup's hair
across the face, in the sweaty thought...

Off the tramps, the casuals: grey butts
wet with dismissal suffering
the sun's charity, the grit's outrageous gall...

Forget. Let your loosened gaze,
a falcon stooping at a king's command,
give audience only to the avalanche of dales:

those heart-held valleys that the Norseman knew,
that took him from the bitterness of beaked ships
– the dragon prow and loud, ambitious oar –

to fiords waveless and immutable,
where no keels countermarched the may's foam,
and words once scattered on a salt wind

came seasoned back, to spice a softer tongue –
with mead in ram's horn helmets, hung swords,
and the lordliness of flaxen hair.

*1952*                     *Geoffrey Holloway*

## NIGHT DRIVE OVER SHAP

The road twists upward, a giant's rope
on the bulk to Shap. I'd left it late
(low February light fades at five)
lingering over lemon tea at Windermere.
Trying to unravel my reasons for travelling
I headed for Haweswater
hidden in its long volcanic fissure.

Headlights questioning each bend,
beams indenting the dark,
I was strung up to brake –
on the right broken boulders
on the left a black gap –
I saw new meaning in the saying
*Turn off at Shap and step off the world.*

Frosted rain bombarded the car,
sheep were bollards with cats-eyes shine,
abandoned lorries littered the corries.
I pulled in to rest the straining engine;
ahead, like pale fish in a dark pool,
the whited-out hills slid behind cloud.
Reassuring to recollect the onrolling
over this road of northbound travellers –
almost I could hear the creak of carts,
carriages, the tramp of armies,
Bonnie Prince Charlie's marching south, limping back.

I'd promised to arrive by eight, not to be late.
Petrol gauge trembling on empty
I made the downhill drop to Bampton
pitched past the Abbey ruins,
down further to drowned Mardale,
shadows of church, cottages, the Dun Bull Inn
eddying in the dead lake licking
the ankles of the fells.

At last the Hotel, like a large stage-prop.
I swayed into the light, the warmth,
seeing, across my reflection in plate-glass,
endless fanged dry-stone walls.
The Receptionist checked my booking's date –
"You're early for breakfast at eight".

*1992*                    *Gladys Mary Coles*

**INSCRIPTION FOR WORKMEN**
**who lost their lives during the works on the Lancaster-Carlisle**
**Railway (Shap district) 1845**

Like crowded forest trees we stand
And some are marked to fall,
The axe will smite at God's command,
And soon shall smite us all.
No present health can life ensure
For yet an hour to come,
No human power our life secure
And save us from the tomb.

*Anon*


**HAWSBECK**

A keen north easter
puckers your skin
like cool breath
on a saucer of jam.

You are no lure for swimmers.
Beneath your surface
Pitted volcanic rock.
I am sharp with the child
who plays too near your edge.

Lily pads green
as teddy boy's socks
pull our eyes down
to orange-yellow tubers.
Hard buds thrust upward.

Cool snake of water
home of sharp fish
and soft-nosed vole

last ditch of sick
and stumbling sheep

whose bones gleam
beneath your gum
and sepia pall.

*1981      Patricia Pogson*

## CALM WASTWATER

Is this the Lake, the cradle of the storms,
Where silence never tames the mountain-roar,
Where poets fear their self-created forms,
Or, sunk in trance severe, their God adore?
Is this the Lake, for ever dark and loud
With wave and tempest, cataract and cloud?
Wondrous, O Nature! is thy sovereign power,
That gives to horror hours of peaceful mirth;
For here might beauty build her summer bower!
Lo! Where yon rainbow spans the smiling earth,
And, clothed in glory, through a silent shower
The mighty sun comes forth, a godlike birth;
While, neath his loving eye, the gentle Lake
Lies like a sleeping child too blest to wake.

*1812*                    *Christopher North*

## SWALLOW AT WASDALE HEAD

Unlooked for – its flash unseen –
My eye busy with a barn and the swell
Of the ridge-route clambering Kirk Fell:
The farmyard and the hill arranged between
An overhanging, dark-leaved frame
And the rough stone where I stooped,
Intent on composition. I took no aim
At him. He chose when he swooped
For the eaves – a fraction of his line
Caught at one five-hundredth of my lens,
Its gaze encompassing much more than men's
Selective sight: I can't call this photo mine.

Behind me, I remember, you
From the south, a swallow too.

*1990*                    *Pauline Keith*

## HELVELLYN

Helvellyn! blue Helvellyn! Hill of hills!
Giant among the giants! Lift thy head
Broad in the sunlight! No loose vapour dims
Thy barren grandeur; but with front severe,
Calm, proud, and unabashed, thou look'st upon
The heights around, – the lake and meadows green,
Whereon the herded cattle, tiny things,
Like flowers upon the sunny landscape lie;
Behind thee cometh quick the evening pale,
Whilst in the west an amphitheatre
Of crags (such as the deluge might have washed
In vain) against the golden face of heaven
Turns its dark shoulder, and insults the day.

*1819*                                   *Bryan Waller Procter*

**MARTINDALE**
(from *Lakeland Trilogy*)

We lit the open fire and languished in
its gathering warmth as heavy rains fell
wide across the hills.  Dreaming through
the infant flames we washed out footsteps
over clustered treetops and through the
listless mists of golden tarns.  Embracing
timeless rarities we felt a fondness stretch
between our palms.  We talked into the darkness,
with just the swaying firelight to cast its
shadows on our earnest faces.  Sleep claimed
us often, but we broke our bread and crowded
all our ragged doubts around the open
hearth.  We took upon ourselves the dust of
grieving;  laid bare our souls in that erotic
firelight and later watched the fluffy embers
flicker into ash.  An ache of soft exhaustion
on the slopes near Martindale signalled us
a preface to concluding.  Clasping final
lakeside hours we came to shape an ending to
the wonder.  Imminence dragged greyly at
our heels.  At some brittle station, we murmured
parting pledges and watched each other ease into
unknowns.  We raised our hands to amity,
careful not to spill the frail collection of
smiles and stars and lakes and sprawling
sunsets which trickled, balmy treasures,
through our fingers.

*1988*                              *Virginia Warbey*

## BLACK SAIL HOSTEL, ENNERDALE

That steep, unpleasantly stony track
must spew water in wet weather, but then
was dry as the bones which strew the fells
and shifty underfoot.
We lost height quickly,
dropping straight down into a hollow of hills
at the very head of the valley.

That high, remote bowl overflowing with sunlight
caught at our breath with sudden shock
of loveliness, brought us to a stop.
Light flowed like water, glistening the slopes,
softening space,
while there in the bottom stood the shepherd's hut
cupped in grace.

*1982*                                    *Mary Hodgson*


## TO A.W. – A TRIBUTE TO ALFRED WAINWRIGHT

Going up through Scarth Gap
To his supreme summit,
There I will most remember him.
On Haystacks, hoping to linger there,
In his retreat from worldly care
His life a beacon in the way
He blazed the trails and led,
Not from the front
Like some intrepid mountaineer,
Instead he tempted from the rear
With a gentle humour.
Pictured himself puffing on a pipe or two,
Disliked the crowd,
Preferred the solitary view.

*1991*                                    *Ron Woollard*

**PERCHED ROCK ON HAYSTACKS**
(in memory of Brian Wilkinson)

It is immediately discernible
this huge rock perched on an outcrop bench
high landmark, dry above marsh and tarn
and, seen against sky,
looking like a giant's stone anvil.
Homing towards it from afar one finds
a green pass between summit crags and
rough rock edges, can follow a narrow path,
barely a track, down to the further valley.

I climbed to it the first time from that valley
guided with group of nature-lovers by the warden
to see a falcon's nest; next time
I came from Gatescarth compass-led
in sheeting rain – its greeting through the wet
(a joyous recognition) spoke safe haven.

Today I came in mix of sun and cloud
remembering him who loved and lived this landscape
(young, vigorous, life-enjoying;
bird-carer, mountain-enthusiast, guide)
who homed each year towards this rock from travel
till travelling ceased abruptly, unforeseen –
for no rock tells how near that green pass lies,
nor when we might be called upon to cross
into that further valley.

*1991*                                    *Mary Hodgson*

*from*
**CALMATI**

When climbing crags
I often had, it seemed, to choose
between life and death.,
The choice was always life
the difference a finger's grip,
a stretch.

What never changed
was the moment of cold fear
preceding the commitment
and, when committed, the feeling
that the movement gave
a kind of grace,
a moment when the evanescent
assumed fleeting permanence.

*1990*          *Keith Ratcliffe*

## AUGUST BY ULLSWATER

On the south side along from Howtown
North-west round Hallin Fell to Kail Pot Crag,
The cars can't get.  A path sets out,
Trudges up and down, distributing humanity
So it doesn't show too much:  clumps
Of folk on grassy platforms, separate.
My children, dripping, balance up the rocks
To fling themselves full-length and lie
Panting on a spread of towels, until –
Pulse slowed and breathing calmer –
They hear the lapping of the water,
Leap up and are gone.
They leave a quiet round me,
Knitting out of season.  My eye avoids
The weight across my knees.  I watch
The lake, criss-crossed by yachts
Tacking for a wind.  Their coloured wings
Flap loose, they falter in the heat.
My hands fall idle, too – stilled
By a forecast of December:
My fingers fathoming a drawer
To find this finished warmth:
Hidden in its weave, will be
My son's back sleek with water,
My daughter flicking sunlight off her hair.
Their voices startle me, sharp
On a sudden breeze; "Come on!
You'll never get that done!"

I give my mind to making
That dark months' memories.

*1986*                          *Pauline Keith*

**RIPPLES**

*At the Farm:*

Children
drop from trees
like apples
when ripe.
Some are rotten.

*At the Lake:*

Summer evenings
present
many reflections:

boats rocking
amongst reeds
youngsters fishing

pleasure boats
steaming towards
Sandwick.

The spirit
of Bluebird
speeds across
ominous depths
here and
at Coniston

where in trying
to fly
a record, a boat
and a body
were broken.

*1992*                                          *Arda Lacey*

Donald Campbell made the first time-recorded run in a jet-propelled hydroplane
on Lake Ullswater in 1955; he was killed when Bluebird crashed on Coniston Water
in 1967.

## THE GHOSTLY BELLS OF BORROWDALE
(from: *Christabel, Part 2*)

Each matin bell, the Baron saith,
Knells us back to a world of death,
These words Sir Leoline first said,
When he rose and found his lady dead:
These words Sir Leoline will say
Many a morn to his dying day!

And hence the custom and law began
That still at dawn the sacristan,
Who duly pulls the heavy bell
Five and forty beads must tell
Between each stroke – a warning knell,
Which not a soul can choose but hear
From Bratha Head to Wyndermere.

Saith Bracy the bard, So let it knell!
And let the drowsy sacristan
Still count as slowly as he can!
There is no lack of such, I ween,
As well fill up the space between.
In Langdale Pike and Witch's Lair,

And Dungeon-ghyll so foully rent
With ropes of rock and bells of air
Three sinful sexton's ghosts are pent,
Who all give back, one after t'other,
The death-note to their living brother;
And oft too, by the knell offended,
Just as their one! two! three! is ended,
The devil mocks the doleful tale
With a merry peal from Borodale.

*1800*　　　　　*Samuel Taylor Coleridge*

**WALLOW-CRAG**
**Borrowdale**

This rock, cracked with a whale's smile,
Pitted with a dolphin's eye,
Shared the terrifying mass of earth
And the iron inventions of mankind.
Leviathan lives in naked nature,
Its crystal lakes, its furious falls,
And here in this place becomes
My own immense barbarian that
In infant nightmares threatened
To crush my tiny body. Yet
There is beauty in this power,
Refinement of the spirit,
Marching on towards a softer flowering
To lift us sweetly to its heights.

*1991*                              *May Ivimy*

**LEAD MINE**

As a boy I was intrigued to read
on the one inch Ordnance Survey
"Old Lead Mine." The map
led me soon to Bannerdale
where fifty yards into the gloomy shaft
its barrel roof was lined with quartz,
quartz heavy with galena.

Why was it that whoever mined
the dankly hidden vein
could daily clamber such a way
yet leave so much behind?

*1990*                          *Keith Ratcliffe*

## DERWENTWATER, SPRING

The yielding shingle
falls away before
blunt bows, the boat floats.
Two coats of varnish,
newly shown to sun,
suffuse the senses
as joss sticks might do.
The sun has dotted
all the lake, like Seurat.
Whilst round its edges
the hills dip in their
feet. Merging, meeting
becoming synthesised.
The scene requires an
oriental brush.

We raise a hand
against the glitter, lower
it, and let it trail
through the water. Thoughts
of men flit and dart
like gnats, mosaics
of Centigern, Celtic
crosses, fishes.
Unfulfilled wishes
of poor Coleridge.

Beyond the lake, the
marquetry of hills.
Stern Skiddaw has squared
his hulking shape,
and is busy pulling
down the clouds. Whilst next
to him, his incompatible
mate, Latrigg softly
spills her sighs on nature's
choice of fate. And over
here, his back against
the sun, sweet Cat Bells
jingles in the Spring.

*1985*       *Lydia Thomas*

## DAWN OVER KESWICK

Skiddaw doffs his cloud cap to the new born sun
as golden searchlights splinter the early morning haze
which hangs over Keswick. The night-quiet town,
nestling in its warm blanket-fold of brown mountains,
peers out, bleary-eyed, through half-open windows
at the wakening world.

Tired tendrils of grey smoke
begin their hesitant ascent from lakes-slate chimneys,
and, in the distance, the daily discordant morning hymn
is sung by the clinking milk bottle choir.

The lake snoozes on,
until a wayward breeze, bred high over Cat Bells,
sends ripples chasing each other across the surface
to lap contentedly at the neat rows of rowing boats
moored, prow-proud, along the piers.

On the miniature golf course,
miniature spiders have painstakingly spun lacy net curtains
across the windows of the white-paint-peeling miniature castle,
and overnight dew has wept teardrops of glistening crystal
over the close-cropped platform of the putting green.

Stone-statue ducks,
sleeping on the nettle-warm banks of the River Greta,
raise heavy heads from fluff-feathered shoulders,
and slither, splay-footed, into the chuckling water,
to await toast and butter breakfast scraps thrown
from ivy-wrapped guest houses across the road.

From these
visiting white faces glance anxiously through dusty glass
wondering what sort of weather waits for them outside.
They needn't worry ...today promised to be perfect
when Skiddaw doffed his cloud cap to the new born sun.

*1988*                                          *Michael Park*

## RECOLLECTION OF THE STONE CIRCLE NEAR KESWICK
(from *Hyperion*)

Scarce images of life, one here, one there,
Lay vast and edgeways; like a dismal cirque
Of Druid Stones, upon a forlorn moor,
When the chill rain begins at shut of eve,
In dull November, and their chancel vault,
The Heaven itself, is blinded throughout night.
Each one kept shroud, not to his neighbour give
Or word, or look or action of despair.

*1818*                                    *John Keats*


*From*
## AT APPLEBY NEW FAIR

1. *Lady Luck*

Grand hair swaggering as rich as malt.
Pink plastic leather this year and butterfly combs
in liquorice colours. Sharp girls buying whelks.
You've a lucky face lady
There's somebody troubled in the back or the legs
but you'll never tell your worries.
Lightfingered nickel charms
charm nickel from a lucky purse.

Strapped wrists, split leather aprons this year
as before Agincourt or Troy. Hot metal dings.
A priestly acrid smoke drifts up. Eight nails stun home.
A stallion hammers tarmac
showing his paces. Tethered under the bruised hedge
unshod, slacking his truncheon out
this skewbald tips a hoof,
troubled in the back or the legs.

*1988*                                  *Meg Peacocke*

## A BOY'S EYE VIEW OF SOUTHEY
(from *Iteriad*)

Now hurried we home, and while taking our tea,
We thought – Mr Southey at church we might see.
And then unto sleep we our bodies resigned,
And sunk in oblivion and silence our mind.
Next morning the church, how we wished for the reaching!
I'm afraid 'twas as much for the poet as preaching!
And, oh, what a shame! – were shown into a seat
With everything, save what was wanted, replete;
And so dirty, and greasy, though many times dusted,
The ladies all thought it could never be trusted...
Howe'er I forgave, – 'deed, I scarcely did know it, –
For really we were "cheek-by-jowl" with the poet!
His hair was no colour at all by the way,
But half of't was black, slightly scattered with grey;
His eyes were as black as a coal, but in turning
They flashed, – ay, as much as that coal does in burning!
His nose in the midst took a small outward bend,
Rather hooked like an eagle's, and sharp at the end;
But his dark lightning-eye made him seem half-inspired,
Or like his own Thalaba, vengefully fired.
We looked, and we gazed, and we stared in his face;
Marched out at a slow, stopping lingering pace;
And as towards Keswick delighted we walked,
Of his face, and his form, and his features we talked,
With various chatter beguiling the day
Till the sun disappeared and the light fled away.

*1830*                                   *John Ruskin (aged 11)*

## CASTLERIGG SONGS

### I

Before dawn,
before chanting broke the wind's silence,
before shadows,
before the sheep's first tug at the grass
when the backs of the great beasts
resurrected in the light
there was the mystery.

### II

Cleft fast in the stone's skin
is a lichen tuft. It is the air's
embroidery: silent, slow, patient, deft.

### III

I throw up grass to see
which way the wind blows.
It is tugged all ways:
no shelter in any angle of the stones:
buttercup frantic in the wind:
wool holding tight to a blade of grass.

### IV

There is to be one stone mightier than the rest:
a king of stones, from which all the land
can be seen and divided. This is the place.
Set it down here. Set others round it.
Make an order of stones
starting from the mighty stone.
Set it down for good.

### V

No mark, no runes,
only the sheep's rubbing;
no illumination;
no face, no feature;
I mark a place
that is all.
I set against fuss
stone, air, earth
being born, death.

*1985*                         *David Scott*

75

**VIEW FROM LORD'S SEAT**
**Applethwaite**

The barns and outbuildings of that most ordered world
Spread out their disarray.
A corrugated sheet leans against a corrugated wall.
An open shed of joists
Extends its metal roof where rust stains show
The growth of unremarked decay.
Tied to the rhythm of the seasons. Still
Implements of weird and puzzling shape
Form random patterns against rough cemented concrete blocks.
The busyness of humans shows its mark
Upon the green hill slope.

And behind, the lake in seeming perfect form
Knits its way into the warp and woof
Of fell sides, patterned with trees.
In vast array, the hills stand in their own order.
Slope moves to slope and curve to curve.
Peaks in perfect form stretch linked across the sky;
Their disarray, named by man to give man's order
To such a casual world.

These hills of untouched beauty wait
Some future age of ice
That with unhurried force shall form again
A new, a strange and frightening disarray.

*1979*                    *W.A. Mellors*

## MARY QUEEN OF SCOTS
### (Landing at the mouth of the Derwent, Workington)

Dear to the Loves, and to the Graces vowed
The Queen drew back the wimple that she wore;
And to the throng, that on the Cumbrian shore
Her landing hailed, how touchingly she bowed!
And like a Star (that, from a heavy cloud
Of pine-tree foliage poised in air, forth darts,
When a soft summer gale at evening parts
The gloom that did its loveliness enshroud)
She smiled;  but time, the old Saturnian seer,
Sighed on the wing as her foot pressed the strand,
With step prelusive to a long array
Of woes and degradations hand in hand –
Weeping captivity, and shuddering fear
Stilled by the ensanguined block of Fotheringay!

*1833*                              *William Wordsworth*


*from*
## THE FEMALE VAGRANT

By Derwent's side my Father's cottage stood,
(The Woman thus her artless story told)
One field, a flock, and what the neighbouring flood
Supplied, to him were more than mines of gold.  Light was my
sleep;  my days in transport roll'd:
With thoughtless joy I stretched along the shore
My father's nets, or watched, when from the fold
High o'er the cliffs I led my fleecy store,
A dizzy depth below!  his boat and twinkling oar.

*1798*                              *William Wordsworth*


## SKIDDAW AND DERWENTWATER

And now am I a Cumbrian mountaineer;
    Their wintry garment of unsullied snow
The mountains have put on, the heavens are clear,
    And yon dark lake spreads silently below;
Who sees them only in their summer hour
Sees but their beauty half, and knows not half their power.

*c1810*                              *Robert Southey*

## SKIDDAW HOUSE

("The House was one of the loneliest dwelling-places in all the British
Isles." – *Hugh Walpole*)

Left for us to assume what purpose
it once had other than shelter;
remote in the bowl of hills behind Skiddaw
deep in its own decay;  the peace stuns,
the filth accumulates, the questions gnaw.
How did anyone manage?  Did they feed
on the shifting view of mountain tops?
Why put the windows facing north-east?
Some say it was for the shoot,
for nights away from the Big House
to be near the butts.  Others that
it was given to shepherds
for weeks at a time, and they survived
because they knew there was somewhere else
nearer the auction and the ale.
Yet what if once it had been a family
living there, taking silver water from the beck
and setting off for a day's walk
to Keswick or Bassenthwaite.
Growing up taught by the hills' silence
reading the shifting mist;  working out God's pattern
from this piece of it.  The larch coppice
smoothed into shape by the wind.
The gate into the four rows of vegetables
now on one hinge.

*1989*                                         *David Scott*

## FROM KESWICK TO PENRITH

From Keswick to Penrith, the local train
Trots through the early meadows;  as we look
The windows have become stiff-textured pages
That God is turning in some picture book

For giant children, Adam perhaps and Eve.
So delicate and fresh the sky, the grass
Loping in long slow waves from field to field,
Still in half-darkness, darkly luminous.

Birds fountain upwards, while the cattle stand
Or kneel for the Creation.  For this is,
This nursery tale depicted in stained glass,
Their daily miracle, their Genesis.

And I in passing pray, watching the slow
Morning unfold, – *Let it be always so.*

*1976*                               *Gerda Mayer*


## GRISEDALE PASS

Alongside the sweltered blue-dotted climb,
Innocuous drumlin, starry saxifrage-coated,
Gives way to a lurking fist of Odin
Curled tight in red rock knuckle,
Raw gnarled and blistered in noon sun.
Cuffed by a manicured lawn it waits,
Sunk in the hillside, tempered
Only by the weeping of a nursing beck
Whose memory of the lost giant traces
The path from a deep wounded crown
Buried, layered deep in time and earth.

*1991*                               *Martyn Astley*

## LONG MEG AND HER DAUGHTERS
### (Near the River Eden)

A weight of awe, not easy to be borne,
Fell suddenly upon my spirit – cast
From the dread bosom of the unknown past,
When first I saw that family forlorn.
Speak Thou, whose massy strength and stature scorn
The power of years – pre-eminent, and placed
Apart, to overlook the circle vast –
Speak, Giant-mother! tell it to the Morn
While she dispels the cumbrous shades of Night;
Let the Moon hear, emerging from a cloud
At whose behest uprose on British ground
That sisterhood, in hieroglyphic round
Forth-shadowing, some have deemed, the infinite
The inviolable God, that tames the proud.

*1821*                                    *William Wordsworth*




*from*
## BURGH RACES

There were smugglers, excisemen, horse-cowpers and parsons,
    Sat higglety-pigglety, aw fare a like;
And mowdy warp Jacky – ay, man, it was funny! –
    He meade them aw laugh when he stuck in a creyke.
There were lasses frae Wigton, and Worton, and Banton,
    Some o' them gat sweethearts, while others gat neane;
And bairns yet unborn'll oft hear o' BURGH RACES.
    For ne'er mun we see sec a meetin agean.

*1804*                                    *Robert Anderson*

## FOR THE SPOT WHERE ST HERBERT'S HERMITAGE STOOD

This quiet spot, and, Stranger! not unmoved
Wilt thou behold this shapeless heap of stones,
The desolate ruins of St Herbert's Cell.
Here stood his threshold; here was spread the roof
That sheltered him, a self-secluded Man,
After long exercise in social cares
And offices humane, intent to adore
The Deity, with undistracted mind,
And meditate on everlasting things,
In utter solitude. – But he had left
A Fellow-labourer, whom the good Man loved
As his own soul. And, when with eye upraised
To heaven he knelt before the crucifix,
While o'er the lake the cataract of Lodore
Pealed to his orisons, and when he paced
Along the beach of this small isle and thought
Of his Companion, he would pray that both
(Now that their earthly duties were fulfilled)
Might die in the same moment. Nor in vain
So prayed he: as our chronicles report,
Though here the hermit numbered his last day
Far from St Cuthbert his beloved Friend,
Those holy Men both died in the same hour.

*1800*                    *William Wordsworth*

## WORDSWORTH HOUSE, COCKERMOUTH

A house in Cumbria now bears your name,
close by the Derwent where you lived green hours
observing heaven in the meanest flowers,
while nature lightly breathed upon that flame.
Were you yet aching for a poet's fame
at school in Hawkshead? Did you feel those powers
when glimpsing rainbows through transparent showers?
I, in your footsteps, like a pilgrim, came.
Then near Dove Cottage by unearthly light
I swear I saw you. You were young once more
when every poem was a skylark's flight
above the fells. Though winds howl at my door,
I hear those lines that never will see night;
they sing of morning on a lakeland shore.

*1975*                                    *Edward Lea*

## A THOUGHT SUGGESTED BY A VIEW OF SADDLEBACK

On stern Blencartha's perilous height
    The winds are tyrannous and strong;
And flashing forth unsteady light
From stern Blencartha's skiey height,
    As loud as the torrents throng!
Beneath the moon, in gentle weather,
    They bind the earth and sky together.
But oh! the sky and all its forms, how quiet!
The things that seek the earth, how full of noise and riot!

*1800*                    *Samuel Taylor Coleridge*

## TO THE MEMORY OF JOHN PEEL
(These verses first appeared in *The Wigton Advertiser*)

The horn of the hunter is silent,
  By the banks of the Ellen no more
Or in Denton is heard its wild echo,
  Clear sounding o'er dark Caldew's roar.

For forty long years have we known him –
  A Cumberland yeoman of old –
But thrice forty years they shall perish
  Ere the fame of his deeds shall be cold.

No broadcloth or scarlet adorn'd him,
  Or buckskins that rival the snow,
But of plain "Skiddaw gray" was his raiment,
  He wore it for work, not for show.

Now, when darkness at night draws her mantle,
  And cold round the fire bids us steal,
Our children will say, "Father, tell us
  Some tales about famous John Peel!"

Then we'll tell them of Ranter and Royal,
  And Briton, and Melody, too,
How they rattled their fox around Carrock,
  And pressed him from chase into view.

And often from Brayton to Skiddaw,
  Through Isel, Bewaldeth, Whitefiel,
We have galloped, like madmen, together,
  And followed the horn of John Peel.

And tho' we may hunt with another,
  When the hand of old age we may feel,
We'll mourn for a sportsman and brother
  And remember the days of John Peel.

*19th Century*            *Jackson Gillbanks*

## CARLISLE CASTLE

How fair amid the depth of summer green
Spread forth thy walls, Carlisle! Thy castled heights
Abrupt and lofty; thy cathedral dome
Majestic and alone; thy beauteous bridge
Spanning the Eden, where the angler sits
Patient so long, and marks the browsing sheep
Like sprinkled snow amid the verdant vales.
Old Time hath hung upon thy misty walls
Legends of festal and of warlike deeds, –
King Arthur's wassail-cup; the battle-axe
Of the wild Danish sea-kings; the fierce beak
Of Rome's victorious eagle: Pictish spear
And Scottish claymore in confusion mixed
With England's clothyard arrow. Every helm
And dinted cuirass hath some stirring tale,
Yet here thou sitt'st as meekly innocent
As though thine eager lip had never quaffed
Hot streams of kindred blood.

*1841*               *Lydia Huntley Sigourney*


*from*
## AN EPISTLE TO MY FRIENDS

Will you allow this hobbling rhyme
To tell you how I pass my time?
'Tis true I write in shorten'd measure,
Because I scrawl but at my leisure;
For why? – sublimity of style
Takes up a most prodigious while;
To count with fingers six or seven,
And mind that syllables are even, –
To make the proper accent fall,
La! 'tis the very deuce of all:
Alternate verse, too, makes me think
How to get t'other line to clink,
And then your odes with two lines rhyming,
An intermitting sort of chiming
Just like the bells on birthdays ringing,
Or like your friend S. Blamire's singing.

*18th C.*               *Susanna Blamire*

## RELPH OF SEDBERGHAM (1712-1743)

Begin, O flute, a song of Arcady
    To Relph the pastoral piper of the plain!
Where ouzel-haunted rivers, Pan's domain
Run from the Cumbrian foothills to the sea.
He loved the beauteous song of Sicily –
    Sung by Theocritus, in that sunset strain,
    How honey-stealer Eros, full of pain,
Sought easeful balm at Aphrodite's knee.

O, Relph! thou were the first of bards to weave
    Our homely dialect in rural rhyme,
    Of dalesman reminiscent and of maid;
Thy name shall live while Caldew's waters leave
Their source among the uplands sweet with thyme,
    To murmur down the vale where thou are laid.

*1913*                                    *J.M. & J. Denwood*


## WYTHOP MILL

Overshot,
the wheel catches water in its pockets
with a flish, flish, flish.
Through the wall along the axle
in a stone wet room
the metal teeth go racketing round and round
driving the belts that drive the saw bench and the lathes.
There is no mechanism to throw it out of gear,
only if the water stops the wheel stops.
Somewhere in its turning is a tight spot
that slows all the movement in the wheel, cogs, whistling belts.
Past it a frantic race to make up time.
Between us we have had a sticking place
where there seemed, momentarily, no way forward.
Freed from the fear
the water runs
the wheel turns.

*1988*                                    *Annie Foster*

**TO A LADY**
**(with flowers from a Roman Wall)**
(Written on an excursion from Gilsland in Cumberland)

Take these flowers which, purple waving,
    On the ruin'd rampart grew,
Where, the sons of freedom braving
    Rome's imperial standards flew.

Warriors from the breach of danger
    Pluck no longer laurels there;
They but yield the passing stranger
    Wild-flower wreaths for Beauty's hair.

*1797*                        *Sir Walter Scott*


Let Uther Pendragon do what he can
Eden will run where Eden ran.

*Old Proverb*


**SPADEADAM**

Where droves lagged and loitered
                      the sharp barrier
Where grasses sang and larks were
                      broad-arrow enclosure,
Where steel bonnets were on the long lane
                      the wire, the wire
Where peat smoked hot on the tip of a spear
                      push-button death.

*1992*                        *J.D. Marshall*

## ROCKLIFFE MARSH

I still can hear
the melancholy piping of redshanks
wheeling round their nests
in tufts of grass grown taller, greener,
feeding on the nitrates
in the dung of cattle grazing there.

They not only grazed
but also died, trapped
in the quicksands of the saltmarsh creeks.
The piping was their only orison.

*1990*                    *Keith Ratcliffe*

## MAIA

Mountains to the south,
the east, the north.
Westward lies the sea.

Gulls bark and mew
as grey mists roll
across the Solway plain,
to hide forgotten hopes,
and sleeping dreams,
of the people who came here
long ago,
to the margin of the world.

Their spirits walk unchained,
down twisting lanes of tangled time.
They are known to us
by what is left behind.

*1987*                    *Terry Wilson*

## INDEX OF POETS